I0480730

DOT-to-DOT
Books for kids

Ages 4-8

This Book belongs to :

....

....

JJ Dot2Dot © All Right Reserved.

No part of this publication may be reproduced, stored in a retrieval system, or transmitted in any form or by any means for example, electronic, photo copy, recording without the prior written permission of the publisher. The only exception is brief quotations in printed reviews.

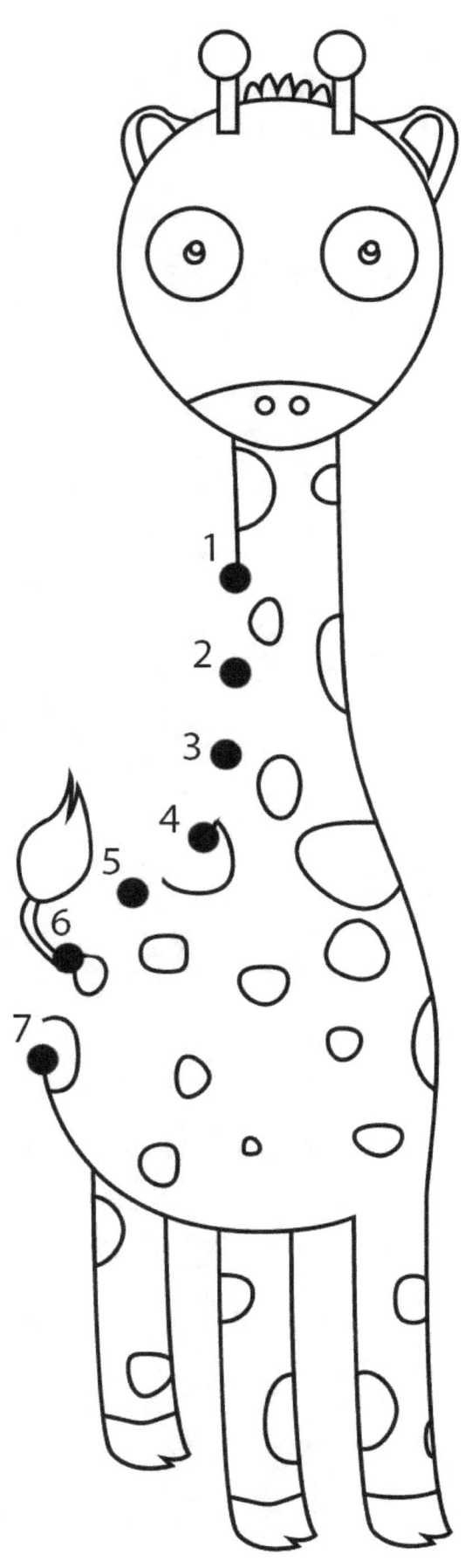

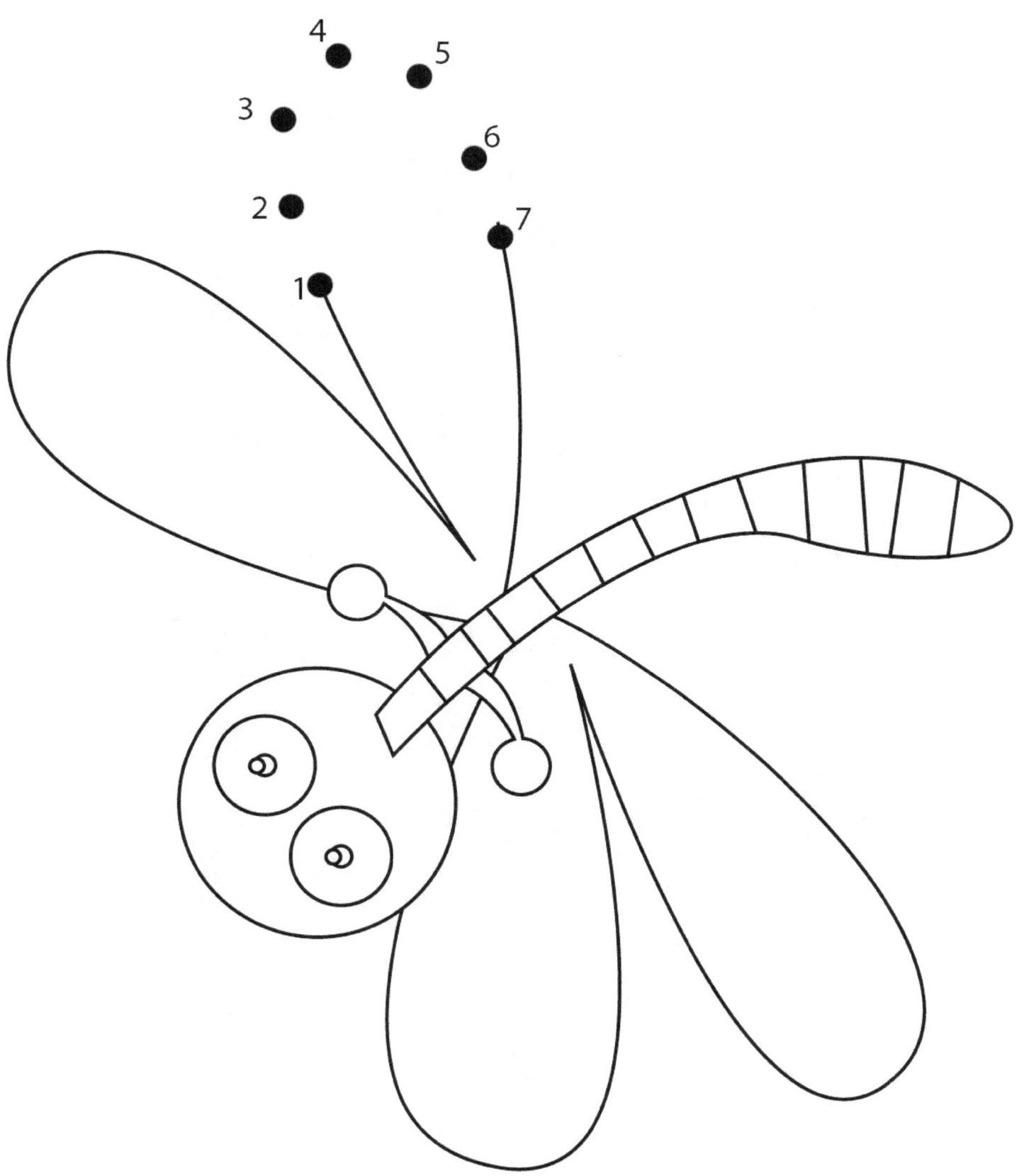

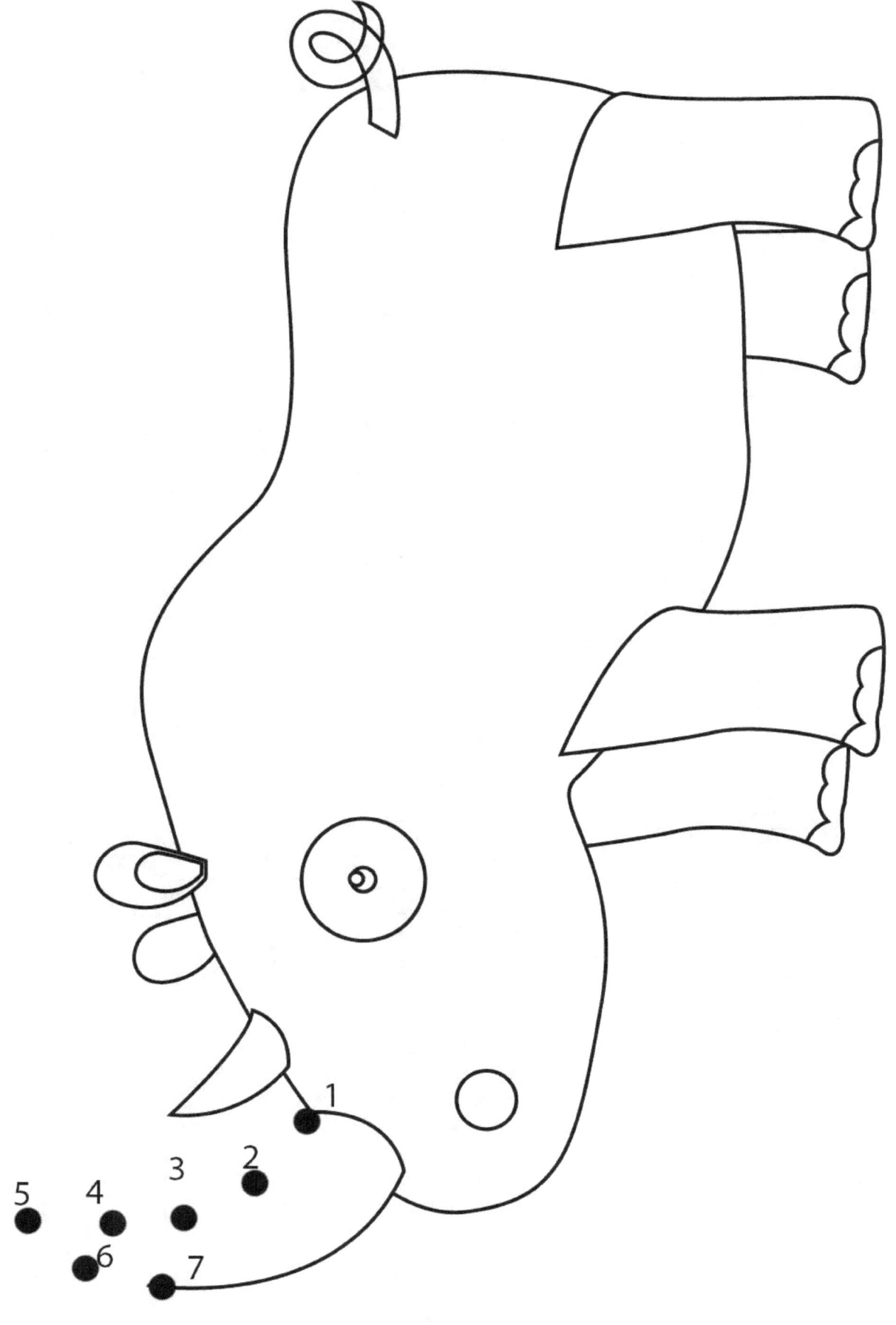

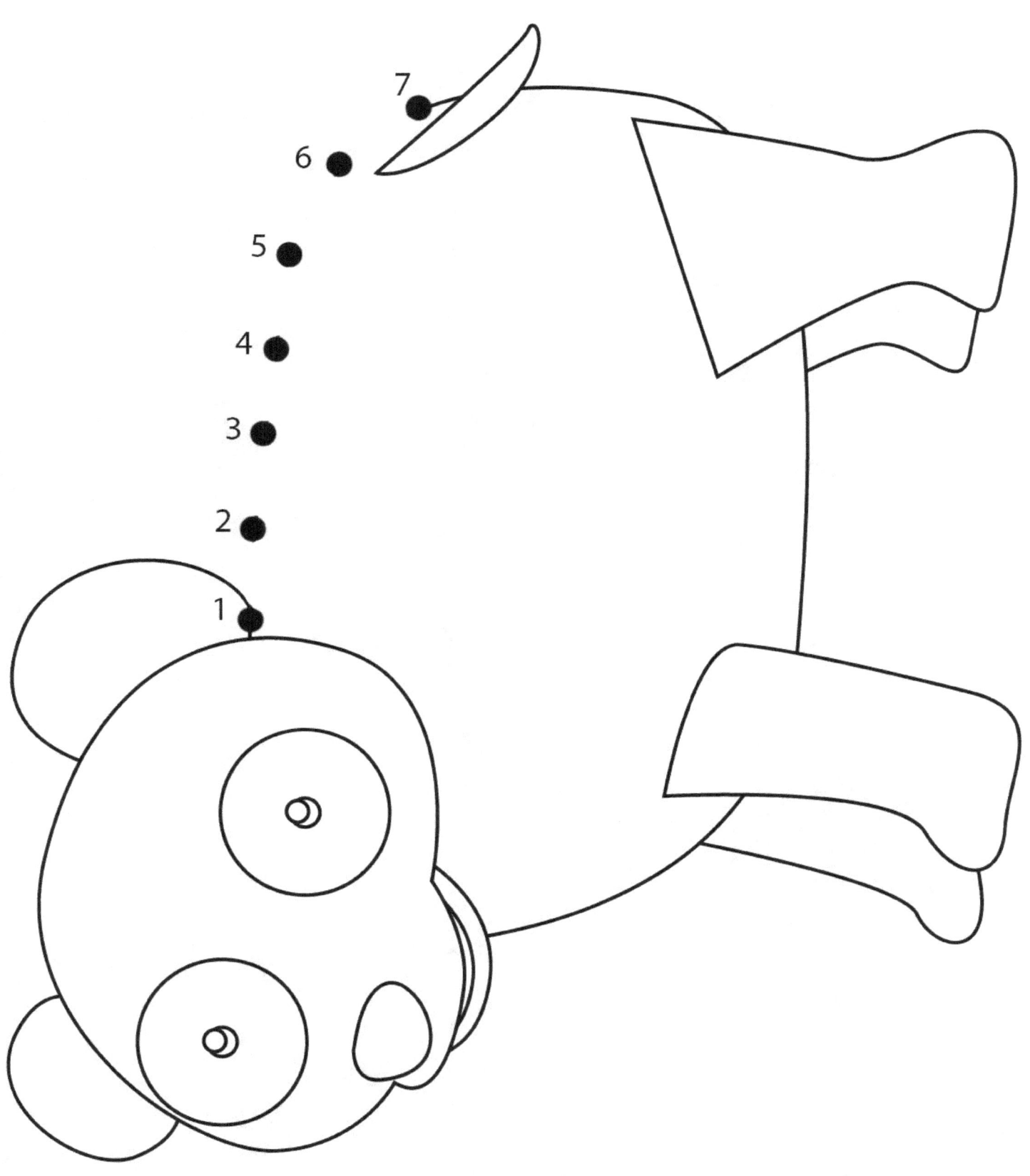

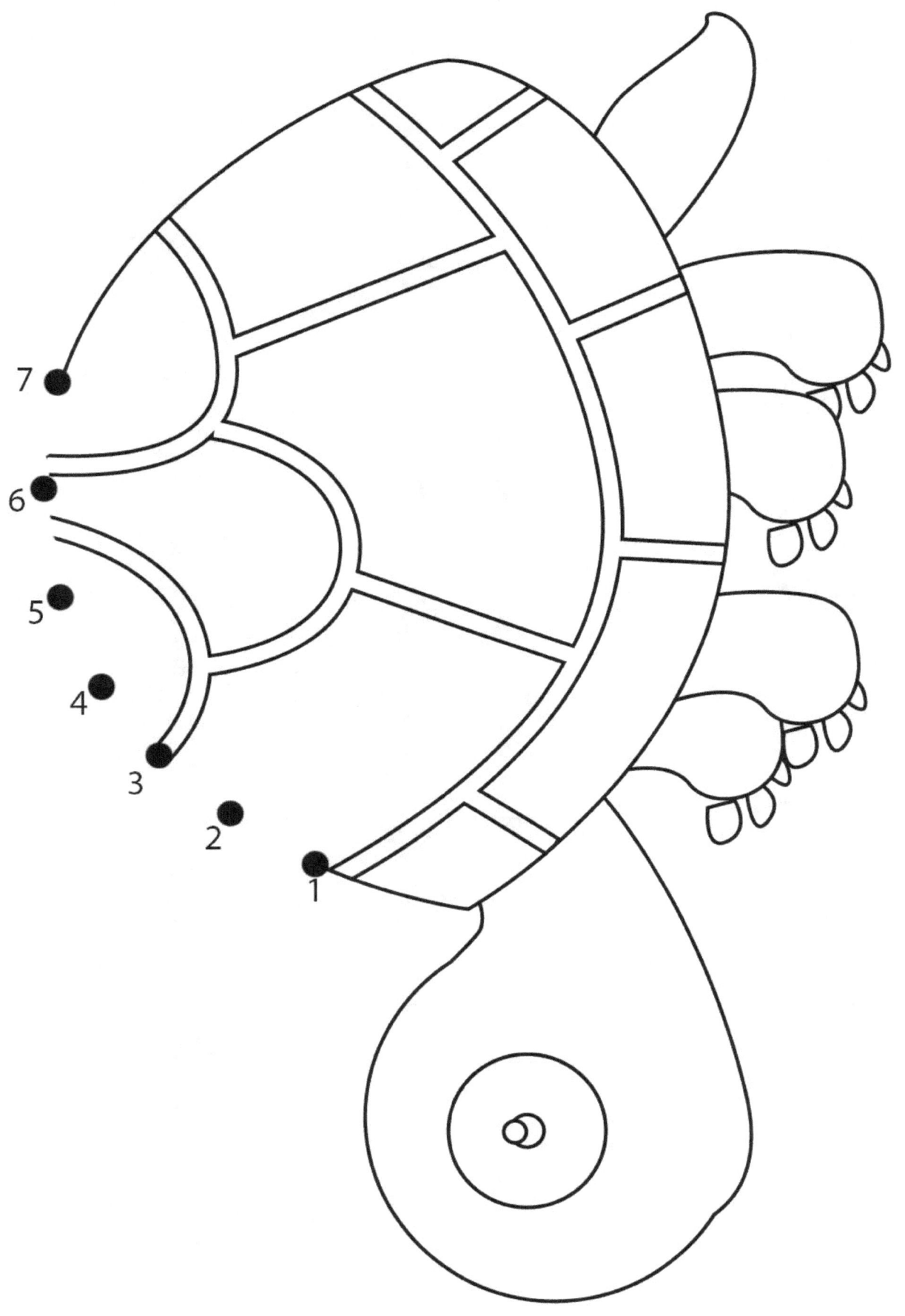

1   2   3   4

5

6

7

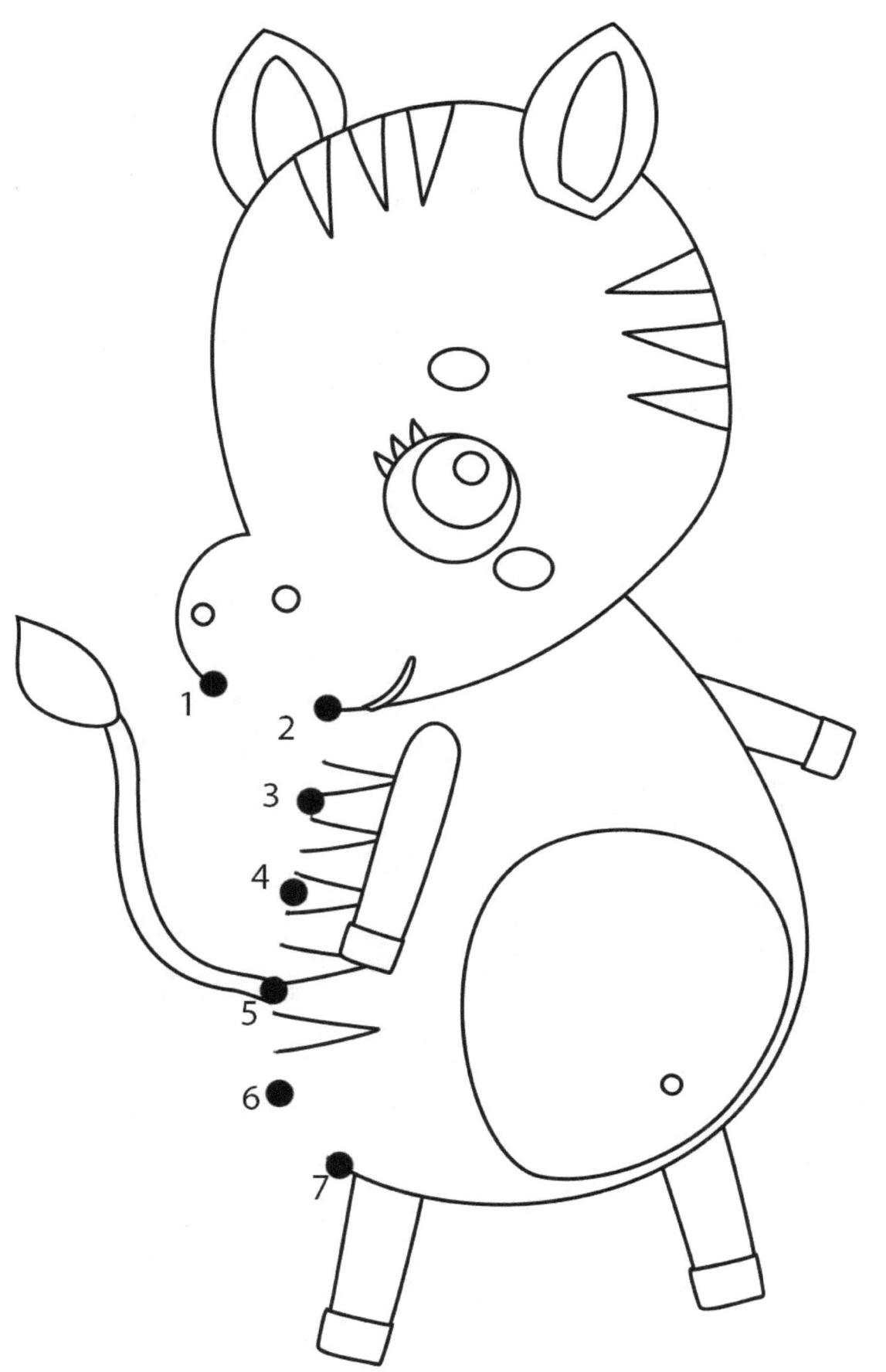

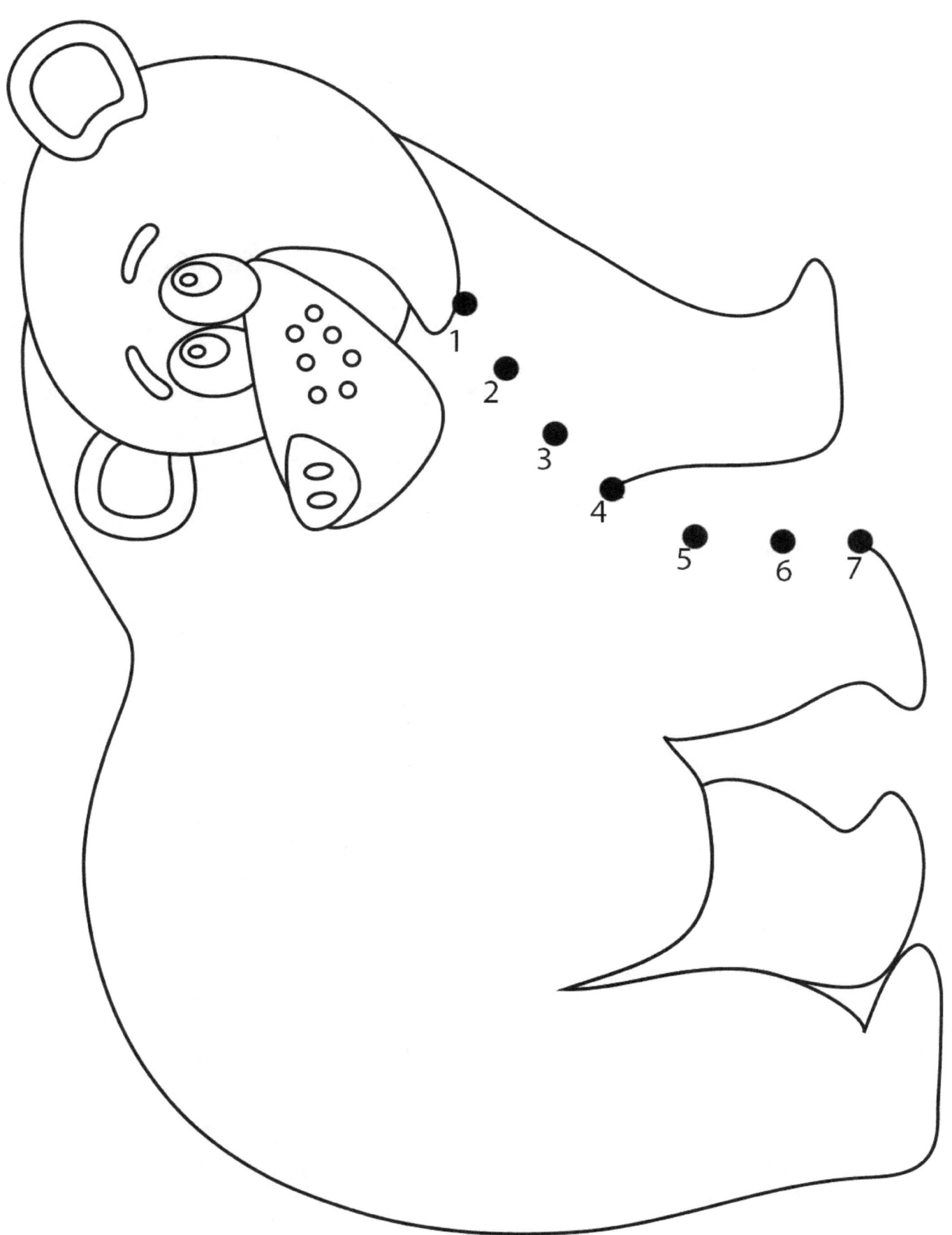

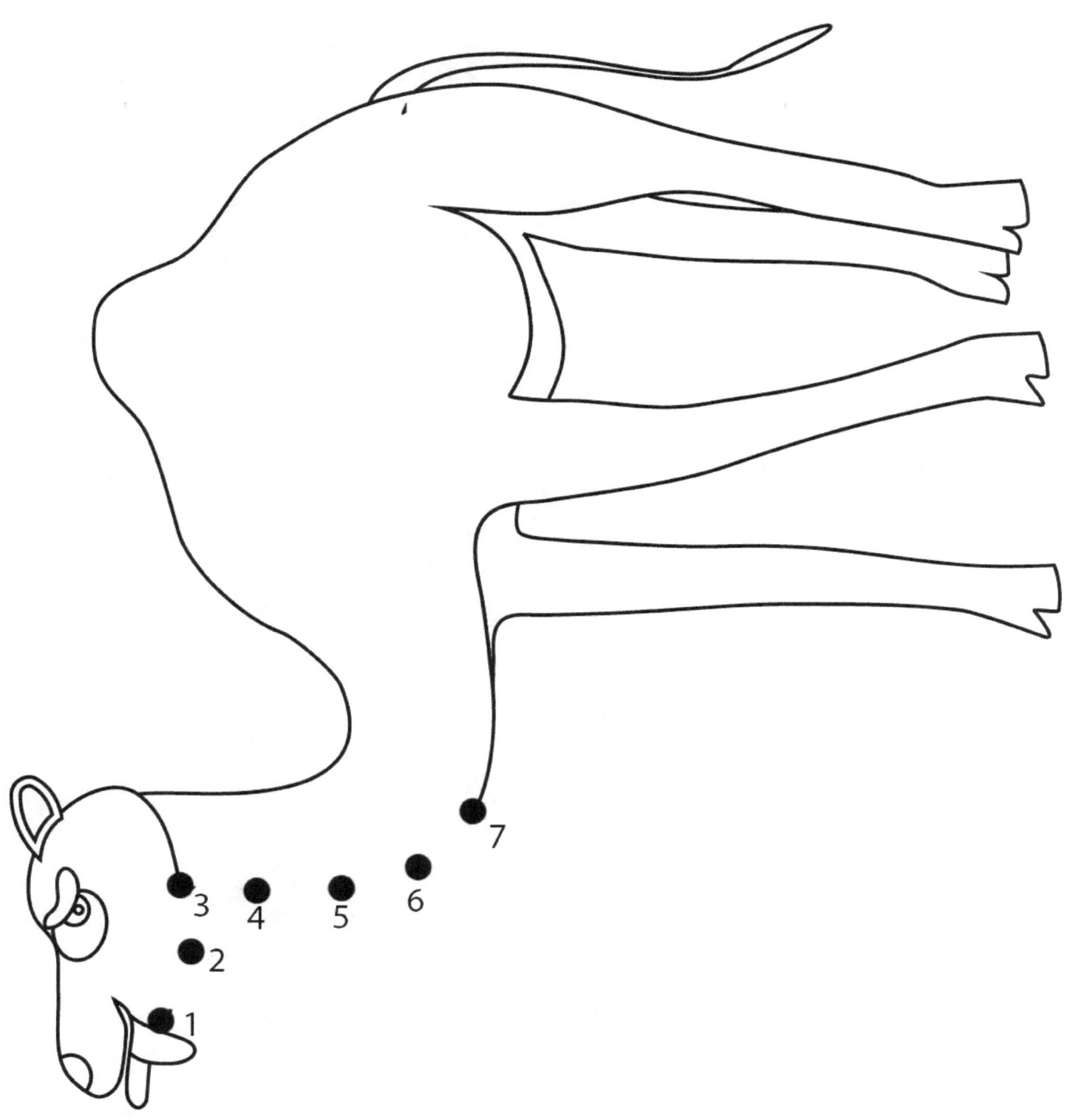

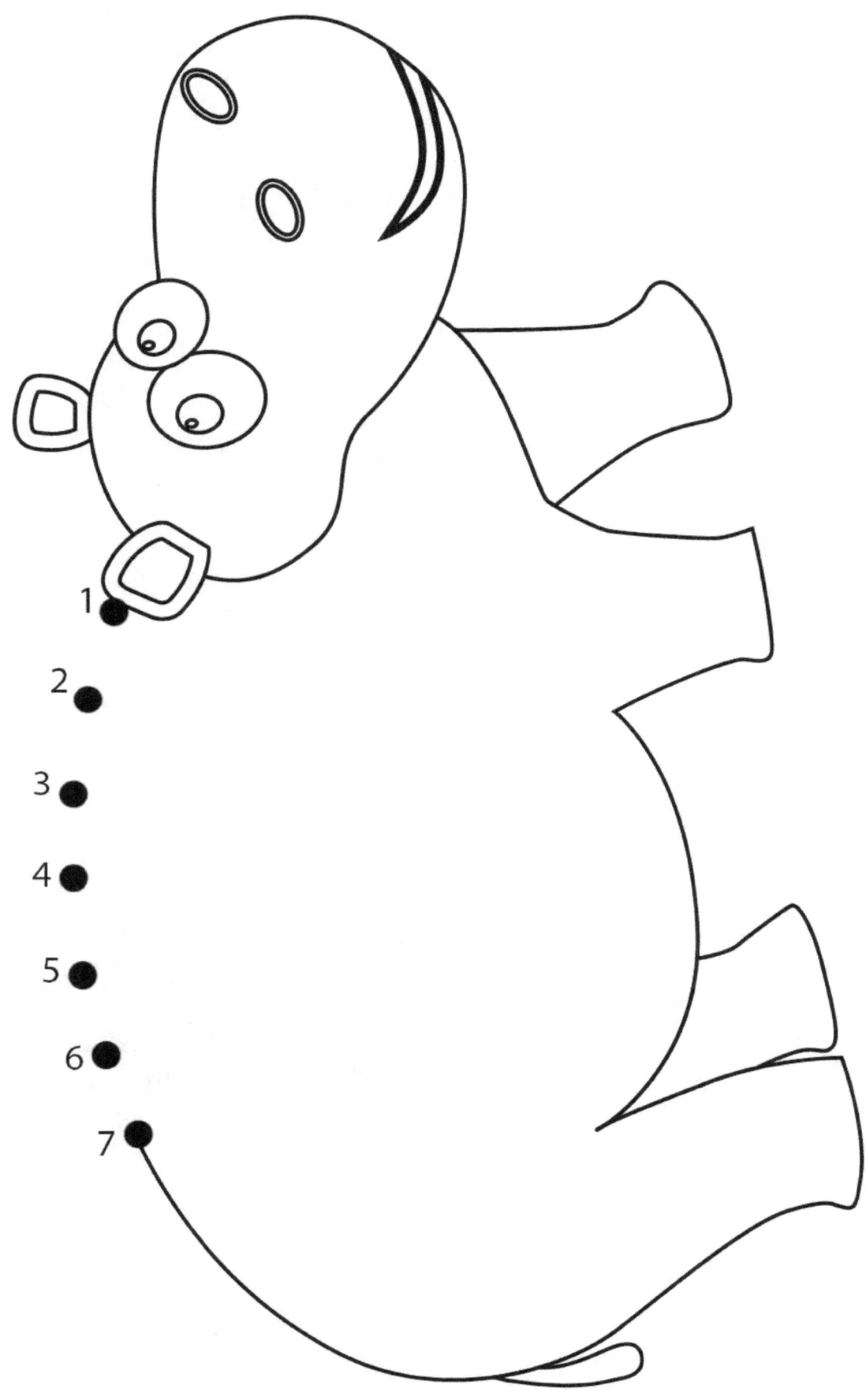

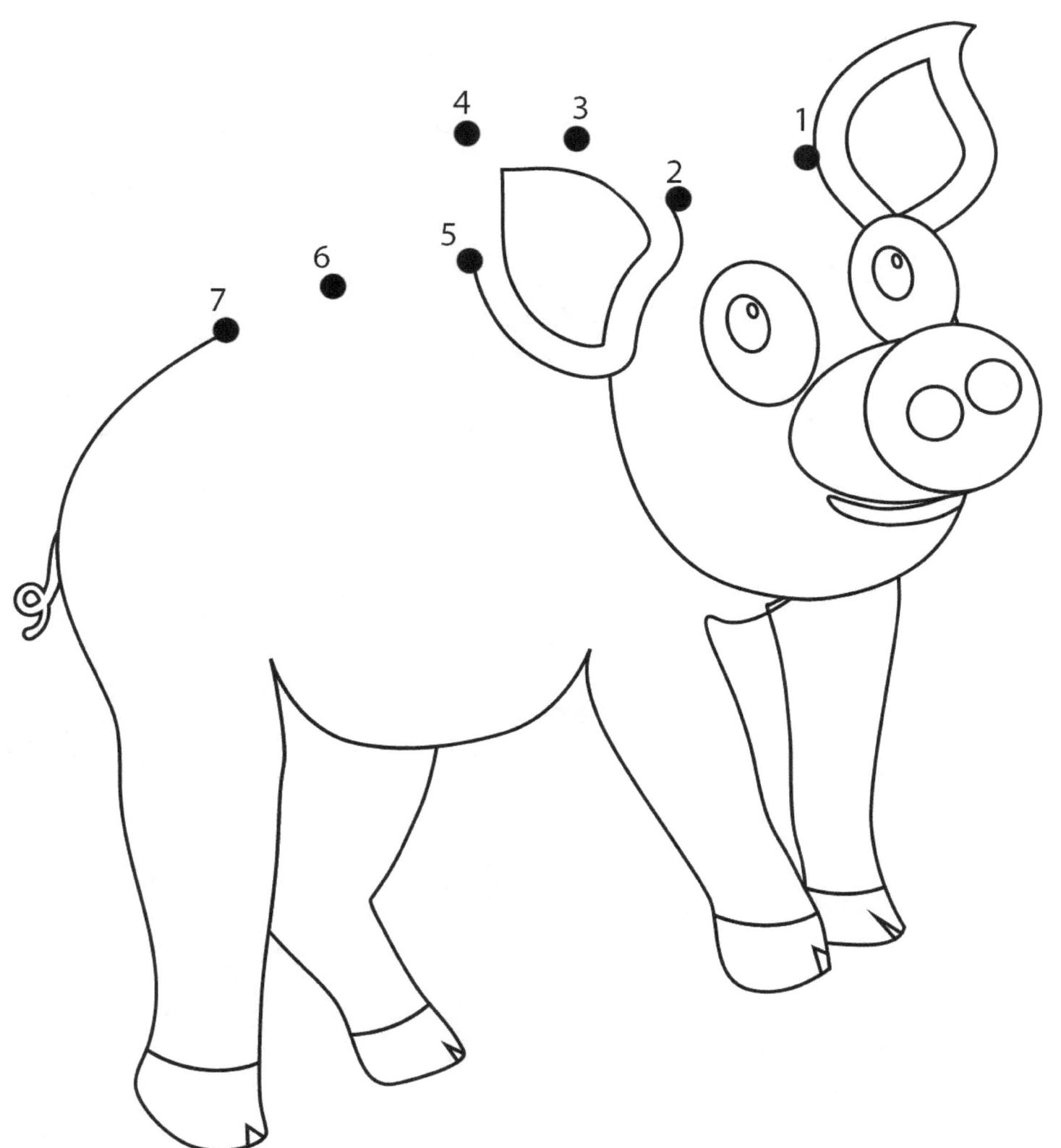

Hope you enjoy this Dot-to-Dot Coloring Book.

Thank you.

www.ingramcontent.com/pod-product-compliance
Lightning Source LLC
Chambersburg PA
CBHW081541220526

45467CB00010B/3285